Straw Hat Stanzas

Mark Bromberg

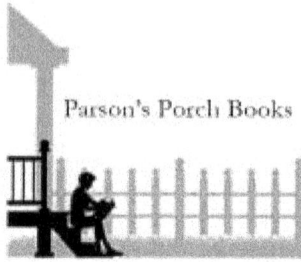

Straw Hat Stanzas
ISBN: Softcover 978-1-955581-92-9
Copyright © 2022 by Mark Bromberg

Parson's Porch Books is an imprint of Parson's Porch *&* Company (PP*&*C) in Cleveland, Tennessee. PP*&*C is a self-funded charity which earns money to help the poor by publishing books of noted authors, representing all genres. Its face and voice is **David Russell Tullock** (dtullock@parsonsporch.com).

Parson's Porch *&* Company *turns books into bread & milk* by sharing its profits with the poor.

www.parsonsporch.com

Straw Hat Stanzas

for Joan, without words

Some materials have appeared / been performed
in the following locations:

ARTini's / ATHICA / A Prairie Home Companion / Bellemeade Books /Big Bridge / Black Eye / Brick / Drunken Boat / Eco-lab / Emory University (Atlanta, GA) / Globe Athens / Hendershot's / Jack / Literary Kicks / Mollyhouse / Off the Page (WSKG-FM, Binghamton) / Psychedelic Press UK (London) / Word of Mouth (Athens, GA) / Word of Mouth (Cincinnati, OH) / Wordland (WUGA-FM, Athens)

Author photograph by Penny Noah
Athens, Georgia

Poems

The journey

from sun to moon
from morning to evening
is all that's left us

that well-traveled path
we know so well
is our only journey

all other action
and each moment's thought
is ours to create

even the action
of no action
as we sit and contemplate

the other
less-traveled path
from sorrow to joy

Rosie the riveter

(January 25, 1915 - March 20, 1999)

I knew a girl once
        name of Rosie the riveter
                the daughter of a Pittsburgh bootlegger
nothin' got past her
        not even moonlight
                she gave her heart to a man
                        who could provide --
                        for a while
this girl lived life
        then lived to tell about it
                then lived to retell about it
                until she was right
that was her life
        she was there
                she ought to know it
                    everyone else
                        they were just showin' off

A couple of children grew up
        or grew on
                but still Rosie
                    was the toughest of them all --
ain't no one tellin' her how
        ain't no one else makin' her bed
                in the morning
(except she says how
        one time there was ... maybe ...
                a key to her locket)
all the other dreams
        she kept in her housecoat pocket
                not much else no
                    she wouldn't allow it

One day Rosie just up
        and met the future
                she put it off as long as she could

but maybe there were
        a couple of kids who knew
                and maybe a relation or two
who could see she was still
        a glass of rye whiskey
                in a dimly lit barroom
                        waitin' for the right man
                                to put his change on the bar

and if he never walked in
        it wouldn't be a sin
                because she was Rosie the riveter
                the bootlegger's daughter
                        and nothin' got past her
                              not even the future

My younger self talks to my older self after meeting at the coffee shop

"... but you don't go hiking any more?"
"Oh sure, the urban canyons are pretty exciting too."

"No, I mean the mountains and the woods."
"At this age it's all mountains and woods. The streets are filled with beasts and wonders."

"That seems like a cop-out for some kind of old book-reading hippie."
"But you see, that's the pleasure of it. After awhile, at a certain age, the fun is all up here."

(my older self taps my noggin.) *"I have friends."*
"Not only imaginary ones, I hope."

"Real ones too. Just because I'm older doesn't mean my brains don't work."
"Still a hard head, though. Putting your head through a windshield ..."

"No, that was you, remember, freshman year in Toronto, riding shotgun in a '65 Mustang."

"Oh yeah, right. Well, your memory's good."
"I'm still a writer, smart guy. Now I just topple over occasionally."

"Ouch. Well, the falls haven't knocked any sense into you."
"It's a gift. I'm still more surprised by imagination than reality."

" ... well, gotta run. I'm heading to the bookstore."
"See you there ... still reading, too. Some things don't change."

"Anything I haven't done yet? I'm surprised I'm still around at 60 plus."
That question stops the older me for a minute. Finally, I have it.

"Only one thing. ... You still haven't met Keith Richards."

Straw hat sonnet

So many things to trust in,
so many more to doubt,

as I pass the empty schoolhouse
that's let the children out.

In time's own blind deduction
that all things will work out,

at night, with coal stars glinting,
we make a hobby of our doubt.

So what about the tin-can trees
and a forest of parked cars?

What is it in our past
which doesn't turn about?

Whatever would become of us
without hats to keep our brains in,

and our doubt from running out?

Star bright

Last night I awoke and opened my eyes.
There was no moon; it was still dark,
but the light of a star was shining
into my face through the open window
from a point high above.

I sat up and gazed at it. The light it cast
seemed as bright as the moon
coming in through the glass.
It made its rectangle on the opposite wall,
broken by the shadow of my silhouetted head.
There were no other visible stars;
this one blinded them all.

Light balances the ledger
against dark and savage night.
Illumination extinguishes all dashed hopes
and ignites new wishes in their place.
At three a.m. imagine all that can happen
with the right amount of luck, pluck,
and light enough to see them through.

After all

Do you know that moment?

That moment when the two of you are alone for the first time
        after all the phone calls have been made,
                and all the words said in haste
                        and first awkwardness of love recalled
                                with its rush of days and meetings made
                                and missed.
All your foolishness rising into feeling and hurried unexpected partings.
        The out-of-town postcards reading *I'm sorry too*
                but never mailed in the rush back, forgotten,
                        in the bottom of hotel drawers
                                and missing their exotic postmarks.
In the moment after all the lovers' strategies have been played,
        you lie in each other's arms for the first time
                wondering what it was that took so long to be there.

Do you know that moment? I thought so.

After all, you think to yourself, these arms are so like another's arms
        (as you kiss them slowly)
                and these are eyes that have looked at me before
                        (even as you notice again how blue they are)
                and how the neck curves just so *(but after all is just a neck,
                        no matter how poetically inclined it is).*
        There have been other lovers, after all, each with their
                neck just so.

How this first time is different.

There is a meaning you never caught before:
        a certain *yes* in the way a curtain passes across a window,
                or how the shadow of a candle's flame
                        dances on a wall, and now you know.

After all those lovers and after all those days of want,
    you find love in the intersecting moment
        when the orange lays neatly sliced
            and forgotten on the kitchen table.

The library on a Monday in May

How wonderful – this morning the library
is filled with the quiet dignity of thinking:
no cellphones ringing to the chorus
of Beyoncé's "Lemonade," only faint-blue faces
staring quietly at computer screens.

School has let out for another summer.
The usual crowd of chatty kids
has dispersed like seeds
to more fertile ground that doesn't require
the roaring silence of books.

It's been a while since I enjoyed
the treasure of books just waiting
for discovery on a warm spring day:
not the noise, the hyperactive children
to distract me from browsing for a lazy hour.

Today, with nothing to interfere,
I walk slowly in the fiction stacks,
my mind drifting along rows of spines.
I pluck *The Scarlet Pimpernel*
from a dusty shelf and read fifty pages
near a sunny window.

Viral virtue: spring 2020

Viral virtue is the thing this year —
keep your distance. Steer clear
of friends and spouses, don't take
handshakes from friendly louses.

When you go out, wear mask and gloves;
don't take chances. Avoid love's glances.
Enjoy the time to be called lazy
while half the nation has gone crazy.

Wash your hands. Avoid sneezes!
Donate money, if you feel like giving;
get 40 winks, embrace virtual living,
and beware the virus on soft breezes.

Invisibility

I've reached the age of invisibility:
bicycle riders zoom past me
as though I'm not there,
and younger riders test
their superhero powers
by seeing how close they come
before veering away.

I seem to be just as invisible
at the grocery, while being in the way
at the same time. Shoppers
stare at phones, mesmerized
by the dazzling shelves,
until their carts bump into me
without even the murmur
of *excuse me*

while I'm making the decision
which oatmeal to buy
from the bottom shelf.
(old-fashioned? Quick?)
It's my own new superpower
of invisibility.
I'll leave the quick oats for Superman.

Hermits

Hermits are expected to live in the wilderness,
but these days they live on every street.
Our quarantined neighbors tend neat gardens,
learn to bake bread, and arrange grocery delivery.
Their hideaways have addresses on Hollie and Red Fox Run.

Alps Road is no dangerous mountain pass
when the hermit goes out for supplies:
beer and wine, chips and dip, a latte at Starbucks.
A mask might be the only mark
that the hermit is taking a chance with human contact.

You don't have to gaze at the hermit from afar.
Six feet away will do. No long gray beard
makes him different from all the other hermits;
together we are a community of loners.
The hermit looks at you – you're one, too.

Without words

for Joan

Without words, what would there be?
      The wind still sighing in birches
          on green hillsides,
the soft summer grasses whispering.

There will still be asphodel
      beneath a sky as blue as lake,
          bowing in warming sun.
Without words,
      these things will not seem
          but only be, unnamed,
asking for nothing in the coaxing breeze.

There will still be birds' nests
      in the black branches of trees
          when you appear.

White noise

Of course it's snow
that obliterates the day
and makes the meaning of time
what it is

stopped almost in its tracks
so it can be seen
passing by you
in silence

stand at the window
watch the absence of the sky
overtake the ground below
the beauty of it

the slow paralysis of time
drifting in window corners
overtaking your mind
and all in it

a white noise
making its way slowly
into this moment

stand at the window
press your hand
on its cold pane

watch the time passing by you
until it rattles
the kettle in the kitchen

whistling
like a freight train

Whitman

This is the land Walt Whitman made
      with his own hands, roughly and eagerly.
            He built his cities of strongest iron,
                  yet with a tinker's eye and economy.
These mountains are his gentle mountains,
      their soft curves a woman's reclining mood
            or a soldier's ease, at rest.
                  He saw stands of pine, straight and green,
                        saw locomotives crossing flatbed West.

His hands were not a poet's alabaster,
      writing odes to king or cunning dark.
            His lines were sinew, flesh and blood
                  were in them, a surprising human spark.
His was the telegraph, the railroad, the prairie open wide,
      and a people with marvelous ambition.
            Prairie farmer or city dweller he loved them both;
                  and above them all stars to fill the canopy of heaven.

When Whitman prayed he prayed to God and Man.
      They were equals. No war was just
            where sons and fathers died as one, and who
                  beseeching God with failing breath,
                      hailed death as their priceless victory. He cried.
The ground bled, the ground shook
      where brother and brother were laid aside.
            No war nor wounding sorrow
                  could stop a nation's building, or stay
                      the stars from turning in their courses.

Now the young men Whitman would embrace,
      each one, are buried under stone,
            joined once more in a last great confederacy,
                  their names both known and unknown.

They are at rest in Gettysburg,
    and in Elmira's quiet fields;
        the places where they died are fair again
            with grasses soft, and in truth revealed.

This is the land Walt Whitman made.
    There is ground still wet with morning dew
        and cities real as stalks of wheat,
            their towers topped where the skies are still blue.
The poet's mark is on the mountains,
    his voice is with us yet:
        his land is ours. The land endures:
            it is our strength, and his testament.

Three autumn haiku

Sweet wine
on a sunny day
cream in the cat's dish

. . .

Words rain down
leave the window
of mind open

. . .

Last leaf falls
now the sun
has nowhere to hide

Continuous present

I used to be thrilled by modern life.
Now I'm not so sure. It's not the politics,
nor the unfamiliar music I overhear,
that seems less thrilling: to be honest,
politics are almost heart-stopping these days.
I suppose they always have been.

Now, though, dawns don't come up like thunder.
Mornings arrive with no great fuss
or my leaping about to beat the clock.
The day reveals itself leaf by leaf.
There's a "continuous present,"
as Gertrude Stein called it.

This is the present of everyday.
I read, and allow messy and complicated fiction
to become the world in my head;
then slowly, cautiously, I remember all the passwords
I need to get through every day,
the real world of the 21st century
I have arrived in.

29th day

There's no February 29th this year
which speeds the arrival of March
and its springing delights.

Already I can feel the ground moving
over jonquils waking and stretching,
working their way to the sunshine.

Thank goodness the month is so short.
How depressing a February
of thirty-one days would be!

Spring delayed by even one day
would be punishment enough
after a winter of gray clouds and cold hope.

Writing for pleasure

"One reader is a miracle; two readers is a mass movement." – Walter Lowenfels

The struggle of writing for pleasure
is a pleasure itself. Finding the right word
will keep a writer up at night
and half the morning while the coffee gets cold.

The radio might supply a clue, something bold,
but unlikely. Television is useless. Open a book,
and a thousand ideas will come to you.
A spark, a thought, a blank page that looks

for inspiration to fill it with words,
and every passing hour suggests improvement.
Still, one reader is a miracle;
two readers! That's a *mass movement!*

A few rounds on my tab

for Charlie Brown

The diagnosis was leukemia.
Soon came the regular hospital visits
and platelet counts. After each infusion
you were alive as no other.
At the Globe, the Sunday crowd
nicknamed you Dracula.

You offered a ride to Watkinsville
with a 12-pack of PBR in the trunk,
and Skynyrd's "Gimme Three Steps"
turned up so the windows shook.
We drove to Chappelle's studio
and yammered noisily about art.

We drove around the countryside
in a lazy arc to your trailer,
with the sculptures in the yard
and the shed filled with art.
You talked about your Army service
and the *fraulein* who became your wife,

showed me the book of your art career
while we demolished the 12-pack. Then,
"Freebird" blasting on the box,
you drove me back to my place,
scrawled a number on a napkin, laughing:
"Don't wait too long, I'm 75."

I should have called.

You had the stroke Monday
while waiting in the doctor's office
and never regained consciousness.

When I saw you at the hospital
that Wednesday, your daughter asked
if I'd look after you a bit: *sure*.

It seemed you were just sleeping.
When she slipped out of the room,
I grabbed your arm. "C'mon, Charlie!
wake up … let's bust outta this joint
and grab a few beers."

I hope you're putting a few rounds on my tab.

Cedric the mule remembers Aralee Strange

She was a good animal, as humans go,
　　　　one of the few who listened to me,
　　　　　　　which is more than I can say

about most two-legged creatures.
　　　　She knew how to laugh, that's sure,
　　　　　　　made me bray out loud myself sometimes.

I taught her all I knew. She was a quick study.
　　　　That lightning bolt across her cheek
　　　　　　　wasn't there for show. No.

And you'd better find yourself
　　　　on the right side of her wit
　　　　　　　or she'd make sure you knew it.

Ha! She was sure some fine country stock.
　　　　Sometimes I could tell we were kin
　　　　　　　to the same Alabama earth

just how she smiled at me.
　　　　She offered hundred-proof understanding
　　　　　　　straight, no chaser. Miss her? Hell,

won't be long now, I'm sure,
　　　　I'll see her come walking down
　　　　　　　those timber-dance tall woods.

Her surprised Wild Turkey voice will ask
　　　　where I'd got off to, so sly. Together again —
　　　　　　　and won't we have a good bray then!

What did you know

What did you know and when did you know it,
        that's the question you will always be asked,
            and even if you never come close to an answer
                that's the one question from first to last.
After comes the obvious lesson of learning
        that you didn't know things until too late.
            You might as well hide under a tree when it rains
                until that gets struck by a thunderbolt and – wait,
you didn't know about that either? Well, that's just great.

Life will go on regardless, and regardless of what you learned.
        Don't worry. Someone's always willing to pick up the thread
            where you left off. They'll finish the story:
                "Now where was he? In the bath or the bed?"
It won't make a difference to them, in the rush to your end.
        What happens after you, someone's always willing to tell,
            as though they know the answer any more than you
                when the doctor looks away for that moment and
                says, "well ..."

Have you any wisdom? None you can spell.

Don't worry. It's good to remember the following things:
        creation happened in the middle of a starless night,
            and happiness can too, if you let it,
                providing that timing and conditions are right.
Your family are yours even if you say that they're not,
        everything being unfair makes everything fair in the end.
                And when you begin to suspect life was never
              going to make sense,
            that's the best sense you can ever hope for, then.

Are we clear on that? Now, let's begin again.

Anno Domini

Another Christmas is past, as so many before.
The tree is down, the wreath off the door.
Back to the days of uncelebrated joys —
and nights with the sound of wolves at the door.

Pulling boughs to the curb, our neighbor comes out:
"What's going on over there?" he asks, "the lights are out.
Those folks 'cross the street, they're different you see —
he's drunk, she's nuts, the kid's a lout."

"That's what I've heard," his wife adds. "They're up to no good.
And others just moved into our neighborhood.
Their religion is crazy, that God's not ours.
Might be some weapons under that hood."

He added, "God'll fix them, just you see.
Hell's the end for them, not you and me.
A politician said if elected he'd kick them all out,
we'll be the home of the brave, the land of the free."

Ask, then, why doesn't it last, the *Anno Domini,*
the year of Our Lord that disappears in a day?
Where do they go, the nights filled with stars,
the peace of one night, gone, in the light of one day?

"Why can't they be more like you and like me?"
She interrupted my thoughts, "you know what I mean?
What is it with others, why aren't they neighbors like us?"
She pats on my arm, on whose shoulder she leans.

Another Christmas is past, as so many before.
The tree is down, the wreath off the door.
Back to our days of uncelebrated joys —
and nights filled with the sound of wolves at the door.

Athens in our lifetimes

The wonderful thing about documentaries
is that they seem to make time stand still.

The fleeting moments that make up each day,
gradually accumulate, become the days that fill

the months and years. A photograph,
a video, a memory: we are transported

to some day that is as real
as that '56 Buick on Prince Avenue

and the girl standing beside it, smiling,
her hair in that certain style filled with curls.

The Queen's Guinness; or the slight of a pint

On the occasion of the first visit to Ireland
of a British monarch since 1911 --
one hundred years --
the Irish Republic put wrenching differences aside
and watched Elizabeth place a wreath
at the tomb of Irish martyrs
who died firing back at her country's troops
on Irish soil. Now was a moment of history
in which reconciliation seemed near.

Life is odd in that way, and politics often strange.

But what unintended affront to the Irish nation
when during a tour of the Guinness brewery
her Highness Royal was offered a perfect pint:

the glass glinted its welcome,
the foam majestic, the depths were black and deep.
The pint was humbly presented in a moment of co-operation
between two nations, an equal act of reconciliation
made from simple stuff, a draught
simply offered.

She turned away. The Prince,
her consort, thirsty as any traveler on the road,
looked longingly at the Irish people's offering
and put politics ahead of any thirst.
With duty regimental, he stepped behind his Queen
and walked away
with a dryness unslaked as any penitent to Cluny.

Marbh le tae agus marbh gan é!
"Murdered with tea, murdered without it ... "
The old Irish saying took on its ancient meaning.
Both sides felt the thirst.

History is made from lesser moments,
the difference between nations
witnessed in the slight of a pint.

Three winter haiku

Keep out!
Black branches
at my window

. . .

After night wine
the room dances
with a light step

. . .

No one to talk to
even the man in the moon
hides in clouds

Chaucer's cats

Lat take a cat and fostre hym wel with milk
And tendre flessch and make his couche of silk,
And lat hym seen a mouse go by the wal,
Anon he weyvith milk and flessch and al,
And every deyntee that is in that hous,
Suich appetit he hath to ete a mous.
(Chaucer, from "The Manciple's Tale")

I know two Cats, one *Dylan*, one *Flame*,
  who love to talk, and talk the same:
me-ow, me-ow all day and night.
  No Mouse they catch, they only cry,
and run all night with open eye.

Run, run across my bed
  and cry so I cannot sleep, instead.
They run to door and sweep the floor
  with unstopp'd tails, forth and back,
until Sun shows the pale Moon's lack

and I myself rise, wan and unslept.
  Then does the Mouse run their vigil kept
trapped in my kitchen stores, newly fat.
  It seems entertainment 'twixt them arranged
as amusement for their nightly gain.

Such a lesson they all do teach
  that Life lacks in Man, each to each:
Cat and Mouse well know Life's game
  to play that all win their will,
and in each other such respect instill.

Ferlinghetti at 100

"I may write my own eponymous epitaph instructing the horsemen to pass."
(Lawrence Ferlinghetti)

The horsemen have left you here,
blind as Homer, to tell the story
of epic days in America,
censorship battles against hypocrisy,
mad poets on the doorstep
with ideas of poetry roaring
like blood in their veins,
while you sat making the minestrone scene
at Mike's Place every day.

Now you have your quiet life for real.
The boardwalk girls of Coney Island
still have complicated feelings
and want to hear the advice
of the man who invented the alphabet,
like an ancient Greek bard
who remains now and forever
leaning in drunken doorways
listening to sad young dogs
beneath the city lights.

Refusal

I don't need any help, Jimmie said,
when he sat up a minute later
on the sidewalk in 98-degree heat.

He drank warm Coke and ate a peanut-butter sandwich
I made from my groceries.
He'd asked for a cigarette and fainted,
a ghost weight into my arms. When was the last time he ate?
He told me he didn't remember:
I just need to get back to Augusta.
On his wrist the VA hospital band hung lose from the bone.

Some folks go on living
until the sun burns a hole in the sky.
Some refuse the help of a stranger
without simple luck or fate
to pull them back from the edge of the fire.

Later, the bus rider sees the empty seat,
asks the innocent question
of a familiar face.
Oh, Jimmie, he just went on ahead a bit
they say, and the rider is never quite sure
if Jimmie made one refusal too many,
or if he made it back to Augusta
in time to become less of a ghost.

You can expect to see him again
at the next stop, or the next stop,
or the next stop,
or maybe never.

After the annual physical

"I let mind and body go and gained a life of freedom" (Han Shan)

Now that I'm older the doctor insists
he looks in my wallet at least once a year
to see if he can afford to vacation in July.

All I provide him with is more gray hair,
a few more wrinkles, a few more pounds
around my middle. This is hardly enough

to pay for a week in Turks and Caicos.
He pries into what I do to keep myself happy.
One thing I explain time and again

is to lose the desire for control
(with cerebral palsy this isn't hard to do).
People spend so much time

trying to control what can't be done
and forget to enjoy the pleasure
of the everyday impossible.

I'm happy to accomplish one thing a day.
I write a poem as the sun rises
and set the world spinning all by myself.

December

The lights in the window
are there to assure me
that darkness is not permanent
only temporary clarity at six p.m.,
and that embracing the night ahead
is as important as seeking the light.

If the Buddha suggested enlightenment,
I'll suggest endarkenment in December
stumbling with my poet's variable feet
toward celebration. I write holiday cards
and make phone calls, share a drink
at the bar near the fire, hear laughter.

When the solstice arrives
I'll be as glad as any to see the turning
of dark to light.
In the bleak mid-winter
when the sun is only a pearl in cotton
I'll remember its great price.

Meanwhile, I'm thankful for the brief day
to get done what I can in remaining light.
In the darkest month of December
I hear the approaching engine of night.

For a plane that disappears over the sea

[3/19/2014: Malaysian flight 370 with 239 passengers, missing eleven days and still unlocated possibly in the Indian Ocean, from an act of suspected terrorism.]

In time when wreckage is found
floating in the water
we will be reminded
how ordinary words failed
to keep the plane from danger,
how reasons were offered
for the unreasonable act.

The discovery of shoes and luggage,
or the airplane's fantail seen bobbing
like a child's toy,
will resurrect old fears
of terror and madness
that surface like ghosts
to shadow our everyday lives.

Children go to the zoo,
mail is delivered, dinner prepared;
our own small lives
are planned out and plotted
fully expecting nothing bad
will happen to us today.

Our ordered lives are comfort
even as headlines remind us
that life itself is not so.
For unimaginable reasons
planes fall out of the sky,

plagues rage, life is extinguished
without regard. Reminded then

of such uncertainty
and each day's unremarkable terror,
we hope for benediction
as those who fall at last and forever

into the arms of the sea,
the solace of the waves
in their deep and dreamless peace,
the end of all earthly sorrow.

Heat index

Yesterday, heat index 104 degrees,
I had a vision.

I noticed a full can of beer
a passerby had placed on my lawn.
The can was hot to the touch.
Was this Satan's temptation
to a desert traveler?
I imagined the beer
had become lava. Can beer
become hot enough not to drink?

This was just a southern summer,
and someone's late party beer
left behind. Satan, I'm sure,
wouldn't tempt mankind
with a molten can of Bud Light
two blocks from a 24-hour CVS
in Athens, Georgia.

It seemed a waste in such parch
not to put the beer to some use.
I popped the top carefully
and poured the lava onto an iris stalk
wilted in the afternoon blast.

Then last night I had a dream
of my calico cat
playing on the back of a tiger
in a field of iris.
Heaven in a wildflower.
This I took
as a visitation from William Blake.

To an old Valentine

The moon comes up.
The moon goes down.
This is to inform you
I didn't die young.

Age swept past me
but I've caught up.
Spring has begun here
and I'm still sprung.

Yesterday I got a call
from the outside world.
I said *no* in thunder --
what's done is done.

Corner cop ballet

The panhandler saw the cop car
from half-a-block off,
the silver glint of its slow glide
rolling up to the turn lane.
He took one step, then turned
and punched the crossing button
with murderous intent.

It was a surprisingly light step, deft,
as though he had forgotten something,
but he turned his familiar face away
from the cop as a precaution.

He glared into the sun, looked ready
to cross when the light changed.
He rocked on his feet,
stroked his beard, muscles tensed.
Of course he watched the cop
turn left with the arrow, and smiled.

Then he spun to me
with a dancer's pivot,
and asked for change. I gave him
all the money from my pocket
for the performance.

Emergency care

One hundred forty-five dollars
to be paid in advance
just to put elbows on the reception desk

at these prices
I should ask more than a kiss

I sip coffee from a paper cup
and watch the traffic
flow noiselessly outside the window

a sudden pool of quiet
lit by bright sunlight
through polished windows

– this is a moment
of emptiness
worth all one hundred forty-five bucks –

the surface is broken
by the receptionist
humming along

to a Taylor Swift song
playing softly from her desk …
"Look What You Made Me Do"

Sunken South

"He would lump the saint and the courtesan together" (Donald Davidson)

Quietly, the gardener works the shaded path
spread with magnolia leaves, thinking of his father
and his father's father, and how testament to their lives
demands he continue to paste magnolia blossoms
back on their branches.

This task wearies the soul and wastes the land,
not letting nature take its course. One supposes
happiness arises from the idea that the garden
looks as pretty as it did in grandfather's day,
and just as real.

The land will sink the man regardless,
the weight of shoveled earth a burden never overcome.
The monuments erected overtop will tilt and crack
and eventually fall. His sons, those saints, will still paste
blooms on the branches of dead trees.

May Day

Early on May first the sightings began:
the face of Che Guevara appeared in clouds
over Havana's Revolution Square.
A woman in Mexico City reported seeing
Karl Marx in a tortilla she was frying.
In Moscow visitors thought they saw
the likeness of Lenin
formed in cracks of the Kremlin wall,
and in Vietnam a villager said
Ho Chi Minh smiled up at him
from the whorls of wood
in his rice bowl.

Unexpectedly,
the workers of the world
felt they had nothing to lose but their chains.

In Mexico City the woman
took her tortilla to the parish priest,
who could offer no reason but only prayer
in hopes of explanation.
In a short while, the Pope
gave his blessing to the report,
and it was then the most unexpected
events of the day happened.

Subway gates swung open
and public transportation became free.
The poor met the rich in equal measure
at medical clinics. Around the world
The Internationale was sung
as lustily as any national anthem,
and the day unfolded in glorious harmony.
On maps, borders and forbidden zones disappeared.

The following day it was all over.
The unrestrained joy was followed
by the usual anomie and mild depression.
The only reminder
that the day had occurred at all
happened on Israel's West Bank,
where a lion was seen lying with a lamb,
but it was soon decided that no one
wanted to guess what that meant.

Three spring haiku

Two rainbows over tea
beat a three-cloud straight
every time

. . .

Butterfly on the zinnia
with stained-glass wings
garden cathedral

. . .

The cat sleeps
birds
gather on branches

Under the bright lights

One day they will wheel me under the bright lights
  and open me with the surgeon's scalpel
    and out will come the valuable organs I depended on,
      expended at last from their work no longer needed.
The lungs I needed for breath to form words and kidneys the filters for alcohol,
  the ears I listened with to be able to tell truth from lies every day,
    the pump the heart that I needed to keep me going for so long
      believing in love and trust in the goodness of others.

The surgeon will remove my eyes,
  the ones they said made me look like my mother
    in the old photos, and I wish while the doctor is busy working
      he'd remove my father's crooked grin too,
the one I used to see in my face every morning when I shaved
  catching myself with the razor in the exact spot he used to.
    It's unavoidable, this genetic blueprint,
      even as I mutter to myself *I've turned into the old man at last.*
I wish he'd take it right off.
  It took a lifetime to accomplish this remarkable family resemblance
    even though it seemed like no time at all.
      I am through with it and will not need it where I am going.

Next out will come my old man's liver embalmed in beer and whiskey,
  such a fine preserving fluid that kept me in friends and partners and
    their conversations and crazy ideas late at night,
      sitting in warm smoky bars until past closing time.
The surgeon will remove my own sharp tongue, the one that spoke
  usually before I had a chance to stop myself
    simply because I liked the rhythms that the words made,

and leaving the bar sometimes too late,
    sitting shivering in cold driveways in mid-February, still talking,
        when we should have gone inside and lie together:
            the touch of other's hands and the brush of a thigh
                better than any blanket to make me warm
                even just to think of it now.

Then he should remove my own hands, first the one and then the other.
    I won't need them any longer, their work being finished and complete:
        my right hand, the one that curls helplessly spasmed
            around nothing at all as though it were holding on to life
itself,
will relax from its palsy and release (as though nothing were the matter)
    the poems I lost and never found again. They will come pouring out,
        the words all spilled from their vessels the small vials of fingers,
all those poems will finally come pouring out in immutable and perfect meaning.

At last, very carefully and with great precision,
    the surgeon will remove my brain from its stem,
        solemnly intoning *come up Kinch you fearful Jesuit*
            in the final sacrament as I lay splayed upon his table,
and he holds my brain aloft in the light of the surgical theater.
    When I am not alive anymore all these things will be possible.
        I will finally be free from the firing of synapses
            and the electric overload of epilepsy-sparking tremors.
There will finally be no hesitation between thought and the word,
    the thoughts will spring from my mind released from its case,
        and all the words I formed and never said will fill the room.
            I will return to the universe once more and become the
            electricity of stars.

For the life of me

Waiting for the end of something
is hoping for something else;
look for clues, or simply close your eyes,
turn off the noise of a dreary day,
and make dinner listening to Purcell's *King Arthur*
with its liberetto by John Dryden.

> *Your hay, it is mow'd and your corn is reap'd,*
> *Your barns will be full and your hovels heap'd.*

Consider the idea of wanting anything else
but what is given: things can always be worse, and worse still.
It's better not to wait for the alchemy of wishes,
and more helpful to keep an eye when dinner's done.

> *For prating so long, like a book-learn'd sot,*
> *Till pudding and dumpling are burnt to the pot.*

New year mess

The morning of January first
I throw out the coffee grounds
thinking *if only it was this easy,*

to start again each year
without lingering doubt
and the sense that things

will get worse before better --
but, distracted by this thought,
my aim isn't perfect

and the soggy mess I toss
misses the rim and goes *splat*
and slides down the sides of the can.

Another mess to clean up,
a new year here and now, another chance
to practice getting better.

Raintree County

Elizabeth Taylor never taught me how to kiss in *Raintree County*.
      Neither did watching Marilyn Monroe in *Some Like It Hot*
           or Kim Novak in *Vertigo*. I never learned to kiss in a bar,
though a girl was always willing to teach me,
      or on the front steps of a house at midnight with someone
           telling me to go.

I sat in a Ford pick-up during a hard rain
      while Jim traced the line of his broken nose
           with my fingers, and told me how he did it
playing for the Richmond Braves in '92,
      and the pain when he collided at home plate
           with the Charlotte catcher, a real zinger.

Now, at forty, he was feeling too old for the young man
      still inside that wanted not to be stupid and not know
           what he was doing any more. *Is it all right if we kiss,*
he said, and then he tried
      to put his arm around me, awkwardly, not certain
           really, why or what for.

If I didn't want to, he'd understand, he said, *I'm not queer,*
      but every now and then he just wanted to hold
           someone else. Said he was just getting tired
of feeling so old and weird,
      said he wanted to remember what happened
           to his younger self.

He took off the work shirt to show me the muscle
      he'd lost, and cursed the scars from years of playing ball,
           the old scalpel lines over torn ligaments. He told me
his shoulder still ached when it rained,
      his knees were even worse, and asked would I be
           too embarrassed to rub his shoulder for him. He meant

he was scared of losing control, that he'd worked
       hard all his life. He told me about his marriage
           and the son who'd almost died. That was ten years ago.
Now he and his wife argued about the bills
       and the lack of work and wound up yelling over
          was what was missing inside.

Then he asked me the obvious question, more tender
       than dumb. We kissed. "I'm old, I guess," he told me.
         "I'm used to my own bed." We talked
about small towns and families
       and fathers and sons, and high-school girls
         he would never marry instead.

I saw the truck a week later where I worked. Jim
       was on the way to the basement,
         where the rain had come in. He nodded too.
He carried a ladder
       over that sore shoulder, his workshirt
         soaked to a tired dark blue.

No, I didn't learn kisses from watching a Hollywood beauty
       but l learned eventually that every kiss
         doesn't lead to love.
There were other movies, I knew,
       besides *Raintree County* -- other movies,
         and other lives, other loves.

Angel double dare

Although I don't believe in angels
I believe they believe they exist

and as long as they leave room for me
in whatever their idea of heaven is

I suppose that's the best of all
possible afterworlds to expect even though

it is very tempting to think angels want
to taste beer once more

and whether beer exists in heaven
that is sweeter to think about

than if existence itself has more meaning
or believing that it does

The bad old days

Waiting for the bad old days to end
can use up much of one's allotted time.
The end of World War II

sped history up a day at most:
these were days people kissed more hopefully,
laughed more easily, had another drink.

They wondered why they had worried so.
Things haven't been the good old days
in quite a while. The years fly by

in a panic, short of breath:
time wobbles on bad knees,
ticks faster in a weak heart,

forgets the quick kiss out the door
in the dash to the doctor's office.
Can we declare when the bad day's gone?

Declare the good old days
are what they are. The night falls,
the grateful kiss

is remembered at the last
in spite of the late-night news report.
Turn out the bedside lamp: sleep.

Make the excitable heart
slip into a measured beat,
call the good day done.

The quick and the dead

"Poetry makes nothing happen" —
that's Auden, as dry
as a martini with a wry
      twist.
      Politics
used to be one of those nothings, fodder
for poets baying at the moon,
like the subject of Love,
      essential but meaningless
      to all but those who are in deep.

Now we are in it deep, all
of us. America, trumped by
the politics of the daily tweet-
      storm,
      Presidential
pandering of emotion threatening
to overturn the nation in a tantrum.
      It makes us wish for the return
      of good old politics again,

meaningless but essential
to the boring democracy
of the six o'clock
      news.
      Poets
are once more "the unacknowledged
legislators of the world" – that's Shelley,
who knew the politician's frown and wrinkled lip,
      and sneer of cold command:
      "... Round the decay

Of that colossal wreck, boundless and bare,
The lone and level sands stretch far away."

Morning news

Only as we grow older
do we acknowledge the woman

at the crosswalk, and how beautiful
she is with her shopping bag

and ancient purse. The little boy,
her grandson of no use but love,

runs ahead of her just as the future
has no thought of tomorrow.

She worries about
what to make for dinner,

how to pay the bills,
how to make the money last.

He, disregarding, flies down the street
in the face of worry

like a spinning toy
across a tabletop.

The world is no better
than the day before, and it is no worse.

God's ashes

I did it. I did it
because God was getting too needy.

His friendship had moved beyond endurance
and He wanted my attention constantly.

Afterwards I put God's ashes on the shelf
in the most beautiful dime-store urn

I could find. It wasn't much with its paste jewels
But still, He looked beautiful next to the mirrored stand,

so that every day now when I go out
I can talk to him while I adjust my hat.

I might go to lunch with some friends, and
then after that do a little shopping.

"So long, God, I'll be back in a while. I'll
 pick us up something for dinner:

vermicelli, a bit of cheese, some bread, a bottle of Your
favorite table red, nothing expensive."

Every day I ask if there's anything He needs
at the store, something He's forgotten

(although not very likely),
perhaps a pack of Marlboros to pass the time

in his eternal, unending
loneliness

and every day when I go out, I give a dollar
to anyone who asks for change.

The woman who jumped from the window of the Winecoff Hotel

(Atlanta, December 7, 1946)

An amateur photographer, a student at Georgia Tech,
captured the woman in mid-air without a dress
in the cold December night.

She escaped the flames by jumping out a window
above the fire on the seventh floor
into the floodlight darkness.

Of the hotel's two-hundred-and thirty guests,
one-hundred-twenty-seven died,
including fifty highschool students

who were going to meet the governor the next day.
Daisy MccComber, 46, smashed into the marquee below.

She survived with broken bones and a severed leg
and lived to the age of eighty-six,
although for many years she was embarrassed to say

she was the woman in the photograph
with her underwear showing.
The photo won Arnold Hardy a Pulitzer Prize.

Secret history

My father read *The Three Musketeers*
when he was young. He said
his father beat him and locked him
in the closet for doing such a stupid thing:
life is tough, you don't learn anything
from books. Joe should work
in the mills, make the family money,
learn how the world works.

This was Pittsburgh in the Thirties.
None of Stanley's children
would waste time going to college
when money was in the streets.
Joe learned to keep his reading a secret.
Eventually he helped Stanley
sell cases of beer during prohibition
and read in bed at night.

At 15, Joe's sister Emily
broke a pair of glasses. Afraid
of what Stanley would do to her
in punishment, Emily took $30
from the house and ran away
to Miami. She met a man
who convinced her to join him
in Havana.

There is a photograph of Emily
in a thin dress waiting at the dock,
staring the camera down like a dare.
She spent five years in Cuba,
and returned to Pittsburgh alone
in 1935. Emily said Stanley slapped her,
just once, and didn't talk to her for six months.

Emily never showed him the photograph,
or the other taken in Havana, smiling,
with the infant in her arms.
She kept her secret hidden.

Space and time

"A zen student must learn to waste time conscientiously" -- *Suzuki Roshi*

In my dreams there seems no time or space
to think about what the images might mean.
They tumble around in utter chaos -- a face
appears that I have never known. My own?
Gone, not to be guessed. A light there, where
might it lead? Do I even want to know? Go
any way to find out and wake before arrival:
a void of time and space and all for survival.

Open door

The cat is good
for keeping peace:

last week a mouse
upset the universe

and found that the cat
would have none of that.

Mouse was cornered
in the living room

and soon dispatched;
the world soon righted

itself again, and order
was restored.

The open door
is an invitation;

all are welcome,
but should think twice

before asking
what's for dinner?

Messages

Do not expect that when a book
falls open to a certain page
the universe is sending a message.

A fortune cookie makes as much sense
as *I will arise and go now*
and go to Innisfree.

What is the point to a tarot card
suggesting fate is something to be known?
Let it be a surprise.

Instead, make your tea,
admit the improbability of life,
and keep yourself

open to forgiveness: eat
those plums in the icebox
so sweet and so cold.

Heart condition

Given enough time and pressure
the heart can turn into
the hardest rock, a weight
made of overworked goo:
a keeper of faults
and unlived-up-to promises,
its beating a passing measure,
a ledger of who owes who,
who did what to whom, and why.

Fist-sized,
clenched,
until it opens.

The heart's true condition,
for each and all to know
as daylight turns to night,
in the forgiven slight
and kindness returned;
to hear the tiniest sound
of heart's ice breaking
with a force so unexpected
it cracks the hardest stone in two.

Three summer haiku

achieving enlightenment
lightning bug
boddhisattva

. . .

evening rain
the sleeping cat
purrs

. . .

Last guests
chatting by fireflies
refill their cups

October

The world is stuck together with wet dead leaves,
nothing can be done quickly any more;
the fire needs to be stoked and banked more often.

My imagination seems to be in fine form.
The list of things I've forgotten grows longer.
Hourly the cats on the porch claim they've been abandoned.

Having once or twice been wicked in my youth
I can now be an innocent old man;
my past self thinks I was misunderstood.

Is this the last of the old
or the first outpost of the new?

I pour out a saucer of milk
and make the visiting cats happy today.

Variable feet

The poems that I want to write
are always a step ahead. The canter
of their rhymes is more supple,
their fleet-foot gait ahead of my pen.

The weight of words shifts lightly,
laughing at my failure to keep up,
no matter how my thoughts
run to catch them.

Mind the doorbell ring that interrupts,
the sidewalk crack, the missed step of thought;
Xanadu's canyons were measureless to man
and a ruin in an afternoon.

Two dogs

for Shadow and Roxi

Shadow, whose shadow advances
before him on the garden path,
is dizzily content without
man's machinery or staff,
sundial, or an hour's watch;
only a need for digging
in good, black earth --
and a bath.

His elder sister, Roxi, plays
more slowly in the sun,
resting early in the trellis shade
with day barely begun.
By noon, asleep; by after-noon,
quietly inspecting her estates:
by sun's setting, ready for sleep again,
where the dream of the garden path awaits.

Either/or

"The gods do have some pity" -- James Laughlin

Either they invented Love to keep us amused
while we trip over our own shoes
trying to make sense of everything

or pity is too strong a word:
maybe Love is a sense of the absurd
that humanity mistakes for meaning.

dawn patrol / night watch

for a super moon eclipse, 2018

I watch the moon
        grow big and mirrored
in a blue-black
        sky
and listen to
        winter
                silence
      at 5 a.m.
              standing
    in stocking'd feet
    on my kitchen porch

This last day of January
        I leave the man
        in the moon
            to his reconnaisance
watching
        for the earth's disk
            to ambush him
      through
            the black branches

Morning routine

The deer comes looking for breakfast.
She's alone, old enough now
to be looking on her own.
I saw her, younger, her mother standing guard,
as she learned to forage in the leaves.
Now the cats' food and water in the dish
on the porch are invitation to them all,
cats and deer each keeping
respect for one another.

The doe looks at me in the doorway.
She steps back once but doesn't spring away;
she's hungry. The cats,
used to my morning coffee watch,
know there will be milk for them --
I'm such an easy touch.
The deer, still learning my daily routine,
bounds into the bamboo. She'll be back.

Sooner darker

Then came the sooner darker,
came the later lower.
We were never ever-after,
we were further farther.
More was the word for harder.
The gods were fallen faster,
words were fallen larger.
The day was duller, duller,
disaster. Our light was error.
Instead of leader we had louder,
hope on the never-never.
And over this river broke
winter's black weather.

Conjunction

"And so it goes" — Kurt Vonnegut

… and Jupiter and Saturn and Smith and Wesson
and Romeo and Juliet and rain and snow

and fire and brimstone and A&P and Crosby Stills & Nash
and Pyramus and Thisbe and winning and losing

and rising and falling and floating and sinking
and living and dying and beginnings and endings

Write it all down

Write it all down, the poet says,
write it down.
So I took in adventures and lovers
and then wrote it in verse.
There's a game in it:
I learned the popular style,
rhyming lines when needed,
but not too sweetly.

Then I cut my papers in four sections
rearranged into a map of my heart.
No one asked where the arorta was then,
the pump worked like magic.
The books of poetry I used as fuel:
I gave away the ashes.
If there's any craft, it's in the memory.
The rest is practice.

Hemingway's last day

Stay on your toes
and off the ropes,
and keep your eyes open
even in the dark.

the world is full
of boring good things.
Try and find the scary things
that make life interesting.

Take the shortest sentence
and move on,
better the sharp snap
than the long agony.

As for the big ideas
(love, and the rest)
don't tell people too much,
they'll spoil it for you;

and the luckiest ones know
when their time is up.
Drink the poison quickly
when it gets passed around.

Rain like this

When it rains like this
there is nothing to do
but watch: watch
as the ground gets
drunk and sodden
and muddy where
there is no grass,
and the pure wetness
melts the driveway
into a river sluice,
the water seeking
only itself.

When it rains like this
there is nothing to think
but this: this
is where the land ends
and oceans begin,
the edge of the world
that has in its drowning
the start of something new,
some new spring
washing all the past
away before it,
to start again,
life seeking only
where it began.

Humbled by the sun

"Everyone gets lighter, everyone is light." (John Giorno)

As heavy as the world is,
there is always light.
You have to look for it.
With the current state of affairs
this is absolutely necessary.

There is light you will find
at the grocery store in the cereal aisle,
where a little boy has opened
a box of Cheerios
and spread them all on the floor,
his mandala of *oooooo*'s.

He invites you to join him
in his joy to keep light,
to make lighter the weight of the world,
until we become light and lighter still
in the brightness of day at noon,
still humbled by the sun.

Happy hour

Bugs are happy in tall summer grass
        sipping cocktails off wet, green blades,
                and the purr of visiting cats
                        is a murmur on the sundowned air.

Flies give their buzz of delight
        being outside of the screen, for once.
                After dinner I settle in my chair
                        and listen to some lazy news

from a bored announcer on the radio.
        What a relief to have this happy hour,
                rare and more rare by the day –
                        not tomorrow's wishes, but today's.

Snow sonnet

The sleeping dogs don't see the beauty of the snow
   as it falls at midnight, or its whiteness so stark.
     We stand in awe at the new-frosted window
       watching the barn as it disappears in the dark.

The stillness that descends upon us
   mounts hourly in drifts
     deep as the year that ends upon us.
       We go to bed. Overnight the world shifts

on an axis swung from pole to pole,
   from dark to light, as we go on dreaming.
     A southern snowfall uncovers the soul:
       The garden rake, left out and leaning

on the shed, has a cardinal on it.
   His red is my heart with snow upon it.

When I heard the learn'd astronomer (after Whitman)

for Sean

When I heard the learn'd astronomer
declare he had reached the end of the universe –

that there were no more worlds to discover
nor stars to count –

that he had numbered and catalogued them all
and given the habitable planets the names of his grandchildren,

I realized how lucky I was still to have the mystery
of what I should do tomorrow

and the day after that. How intriguing
the uncertainty of the here and now,

undefined and with days still unnumbered,
still to be able to gaze up

even at the numbered stars
thinking there must be one he missed.

That one's mine.

Gilt edge

for Piet Hein

A gilded
youth

the gilded
truth

a gilded
tooth

and not too
late

at any
rate

the gilded
gate

A note of thanks

Poets are usually thought of as solitary souls: on the page, the stage, or as they scribble away in a lonely garret. In my case, especially, I am lucky to be supported in my writing by a cast of characters who deserve as much credit for my creative efforts as any muse kicking me out of bed at midnight to write the words down.

Without the love for the word and the friendship of Aralee Strange (1943-2013), there would never have been a need to write this note. Thank you, Aralee, for all your guidance and for your creative spirit that continues to inspire us all.

To all the writers and generous spoken word community Aralee founded at Word of Mouth in Athens, Georgia, thanks for providing the time and the place to practice my thinking and improve my drinking at Globe Athens on a monthly basis. I feel lucky to be among such a talented and supportive group of poets, performers, pranksters and philosophers. Thanks, all!

To Michelle Castleberry and the freewheeling gang at Firemouth Salon, what a rare opportunity to play with words and be given the chance to "follow my muse, my nose, and sometimes my muse's nose" (thanks to Ed McClanahan for that bit of writerly wisdom). Creative anxiety has seldom been such fun. Thank you!

An extra round of Donderos' Kitchen caffeine and pastries for the sharp wits and even sharper observations of Eugene Bianchi, Robert Ambrose Jr., David Oates, Penny Noah, Sharon McCoy, Sam Lane, Charley Seagraves and Greg de Rocher. Extra thanks to Penny Noah for capturing the writer in a portrait with some of his muses at Donderos' Kitchen!

Grady Thrasher and Kathy Prescott, thanks for welcoming me into the Athens community. Steve Maurer, I appreciate the years of friendship and support since our days at Syracuse University. That money you gave me for my hitchhiking adventure to Georgia went a long way! I arrived in Atlanta on July 4, 1976 and decided to stay. To Sean Peters, who rode shotgun on some of these poems with Bulleit in hand, I hope we can share a whiskey season here in town, the invitation still stands. A chorus of "Irish Rover" and a round of Guinness for Dac, Pick, and all the Sunday crew at the Globe.

Finally, all good thoughts and best wishes to the periodicals, online sites, and other media from San Francisco to London, New York to Lake Wobegon, that have published my written work in various guises. It's a great way to travel.

Mark Bromberg / Athens Georgia / September 2022

www.ingramcontent.com/pod-product-compliance
Lightning Source LLC
Chambersburg PA
CBHW071745090426
42738CB00011B/2570